**arts of
wood**

arts

# of wood

by christine price

CHARLES SCRIBNER'S SONS
NEW YORK

Illustration on page 1:
LADLE FOR FEASTS
Alaska, Tlingit people (*See page 35*)
Page 2-3: **LIME CONTAINER**
AND LIME STICKS
Bellona, Solomon Islands (*See page 56*)

Copyright © 1976 Christine Price

Library of Congress, Cataloging in Publication Data
Price, Christine, 1928-
   Arts of wood.
   SUMMARY: An illustrated survey of everyday wooden artwork
made by various cultures.
    1.   Wood-carving, Primitive—History—Juvenile literature.
2.   Wood-carving—History—Juvenile literature. [1.   Wood-
carving—History] I. Title.
NK9706.P74   736′.4   76-13886
ISBN 0-684.-14665-7

This book published simultaneously in the United States of America
and in Canada—Copyright under the Berne Convention

1 3 5 7 9 11 13 15 17 19 MD/C 20 18 16 14 12 10 8 6 4 2

Printed in the United States of America

MARRIAGE CUP
Taiwan,
Paiwan people
(*See page 28*)

looking at the woodcarvings in this book, you will find that each is labeled with the name of the country it comes from, and usually with the name of the carver's people. We rarely know the name of the wood-carver himself. He is seldom well known outside his home. Perhaps he lives in a small village, far from any road, or he may have died long ago and lives only in the memories of his people. Yet these unknown artists speak to us through the work of their hands, and this book is for them—for all the wood-carvers, of past and present, whose work is pictured here.

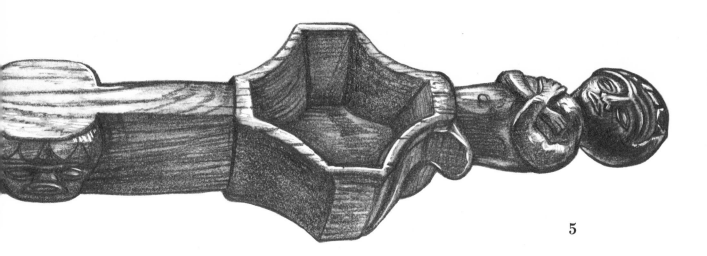

contents

Opposite:
RICE TRAY
Surinam,
Djuka people
(See page 38)

6

**arts of
wood**

WOOD-CARVER'S MALLET
Trobriand Islands,
Papua New Guinea

8

in the old time, a man had to be

good at many things. He had to be a good farmer and hunter and fisherman so that he could feed his family; a good warrior so that he could protect them; and a good wood-carver so that he could make a canoe, build a house, and carve all the things that his family needed."

An old man is speaking, a man of the Solomon Islands. We are sitting in his house on the island of Roviana while the rain patters on the palm-thatched roof. The slender poles that support the thatch have been smoked to a glossy black by the cooking fire on the earth floor.

Above:
BOWL INLAID WITH SHELL
Santa Ana,
Solomon Islands

As we talk, the old man and I, we can look out through the open end of the house at the slender trunks of coconut palms, the wet shining bushes, and the fringe of the green forest that covers the backbone of the island. The houses of the village are strung out along the low-lying shore, and dugout canoes are drawn up on the beach like sleeping seabirds beside the great lagoon.

"Do people still carve wooden things?" I ask. "Like bowls and spoons to use in the house?"

"We still make these," the old man says, "for mixing taro pudding."

He shows me two rough wooden mortars, one tall and cylindrical, the other long-shaped. The wooden pestle for pounding the cooked taro into a soft mash is smooth and shiny from much handling.

"I made these for my wife," he says. "In my father's time these things would be inlaid with shell from the reef, like the food bowls they used to make. Every man in those days knew the best wood to cut in the bush for making bowls or building houses or whatever he wanted to do. Each part of a house frame needs a different wood. Then it lasts for years."

The old man pokes in a cloth bag to find the makings of a chew of betel nut, and I look out again at the dripping trees along the forest's edge.

All over the world, where men and trees have come together, people have used wood for making things. Long before they had iron tools men felled trees with stone axes. They shaped and carved the wood with knives and adzes of stone, bone, and sharp-edged shell.

Wonderful things were made from wood by the peoples of the Pacific, Asia, Africa, and the Americas. There were statues and masks and mighty drums, splendid war-canoes and housefronts gloriously carved. But side by side with these great arts of wood were the smaller ones, the everyday wooden-wares, often made by the man of the house for his own family. The home craftsmen had many skills, as the old man of Roviana had told me, and they were wise in the ways of wood. Even the tools they made for themselves were good to look at as well as good to use.

An African carver made the haft of his adze in a graceful curve to fit his hand. Then he shaped the top in the form of an animal's head that held the thin iron blade in its teeth.

11

The wood-carver's mallet on Page 8, battered and scarred with hard hammering, has a handgrip carved like the beak of a canoe. The pattern is the same as on the famous seafaring canoes of the Trobriand Islands where the tool was made and used.

An American Indian artist might adorn the wooden shafts of his paintbrushes with tiny figures, or carve the head of a wolf on the handle of his adze.

The keen iron blade of this adze was made from a white man's axehead. Iron tools were a blessing to the wood-carver. Africans knew, a thousand years ago, how to dig iron from the earth and work it into

CARVER'S ADZE
British Columbia, Nootka people

tools and weapons, but iron was brought to the Pacific peoples by white men. The Indians of the Northwest Coast had obtained small amounts of iron through trade with their neighbors; the Pacific islanders, scattered over the great sea, were still in the Stone Age when the white men invaded their world. The islanders were quick to see the benefits of iron. Armed with iron tools, both Indian and Pacific island artists enriched their work with finer decoration, and some made elaborate carvings as "curios" to sell to white men.

The Pacific peoples were glad to trade their carvings for metal pots and pans and other Western goods, but they still needed the old arts of wood. Craftsmen still made bowls, spoons, and all the woodenwares that the old man of Roviana remembers from his father's time.

The old man would look kindly on the arts of wood that we shall see in this book. They would remind him of the days when even mortars for taro pudding were made beautiful.

Some people in Western countries, who think of art as a painting or a sculpture by a famous artist,

13

would hesitate to use the word "art" for everyday woodenwares. The people who made these things would not have called them art either, but for a very different reason. Many peoples have no word for "art" in their languages. Art, for them, is not separate from life. The skilled carver may be respected by his neighbors for his good work, but the things he makes are simply necessities for proper living. Even the most beautifully decorated feast bowls were made to be used. We find them smoothed and mellowed by the touch of many hands.

All these arts of wood invite us also to reach out and touch, to explore the carved shapes with our fingers as well as our eyes. We need to feel the texture and the weight, and even to breathe the smell that lingers in the wood.

The people who made these things, and took joy in the making, often had a hard struggle to live, whether they were Eskimos in the long darkness of the Arctic winter, or African herdsmen scorched by the summer sun. The names of the carvers, remembered by their own folk, are not signed on their work. We know they were nearly always men. Women's work was in pottery, weaving, and other arts.

With the carver's skill, passed down from father to son, came reverence and respect for the wood. Often, before a man felled a tree in the forest, he would ask forgiveness and make sacrifice to the spirit

DOUBLE BOWL
Malaita,
Solomon Islands

FOOD BOWL
Philippines,
Ifugao people

of the tree. As he chopped the first rough form of
bowl or stool from a block of wood, the cuts of his
adze were guided by the old wisdom he had learned
as a boy. The shapes he carved grew out of the needs
and customs of his people, but also out of the wood
itself, the swirl of the grain, the life-forms of the
living tree.

15

bowls to hold food or drink are often made from burls, the large swellings that grow on the trunks of hardwood trees. A burl forms where a branch has broken off or the tree has been injured. The little bowl above shows the natural irregular shape of a hollowed-out burl; the big Indian bowl

16

has been carved into a fine round form. American Indians of the forest tribes knew that the twisted, knotted grain of a burl made a long-lasting bowl that would not shrink or leak if it were used to hold liquids.

When a bowl is carved from a length of wood with the grain running from end to end, the shape may be oval or even oblong. The Turkana people of East Africa make bowls of a unique shape, rounded at the bottom and oblong at the top.

FOOD BOWLS
Right: **Kenya,**
Turkana people
Below: **Tami Islands,**
Papua New Guinea

This large Turkana bowl is for mixing and drinking fresh milk and blood, the main food of the warriors. The blood is drawn from the necks of living cattle, but without harming them, for the Turkana love their cattle.

There are many ways to decorate the simple shape of a bowl. An Alaskan Eskimo, using driftwood to make an oval bowl, inlaid it with pieces of bone and painted a mythical creature inside. The maker of the round bowl, a Fulani of West Africa, decorated it with carving, but this is almost completely hidden until you turn the bowl upside down.

BOWL
Kenya,
Turkana people

18

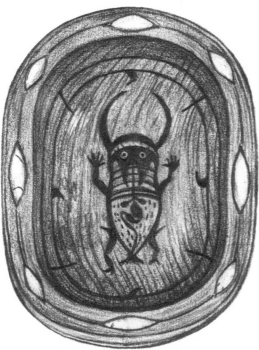

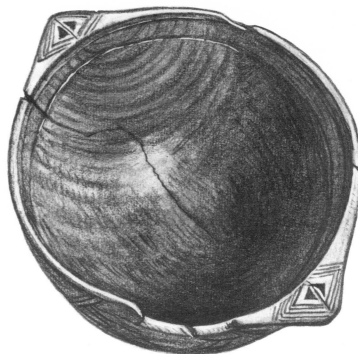

Above: BOWL INLAID
WITH BONE
Alaska, Eskimo
Right: MILK BOWL
West Africa,
Fulani people

OUTSIDE OF THE FULANI BOWL (*Page 19*)

The inside of a food bowl is best left plain and smooth. The outside is the place for decoration, whether the carver makes a geometric pattern or a swirling animal design.

Sometimes the bowl itself is carved in an animal shape. The American Indians of the Northwest Coast excelled in making bowls that were birds, seals, bears, or whales, the wild creatures the Indians hunted on land and sea.

CARVED BOWL WITH FROG DESIGN
Lake Sentani,
Papua New Guinea

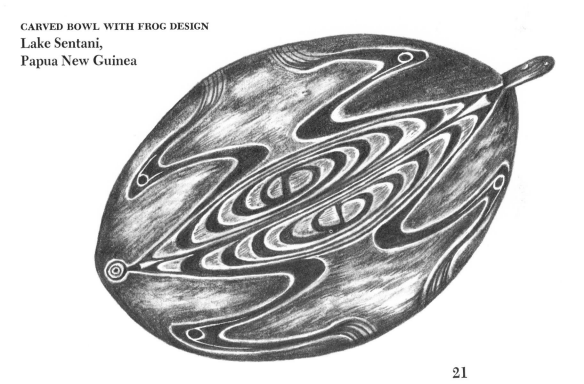

ANIMAL-SHAPED BOWLS
Alaska, Tlingit people

22

The whale-shaped feast dish was made in memory of the exploits of Kula, a famous Indian whale-hunter. Whale and man are carved from a single log of cedar, the long-lasting wood the Indians used for making their great totem poles.

The small bird bowl held fish oil, into which dried food was dipped at meals, and the oil still oozes from the wood. The Indian artists worked with a deep knowledge of the animals they carved. Even the tiny dish with the head of a bear suggests a fat bear lying on his back.

FEAST DISH
Northwest Coast Indian

A carved human figure with the body hollowed out may also serve as a bowl, but more often we see two figures holding a bowl between them. This idea seems to have spread far and wide. One of the bowls opposite was made by an Eskimo in Alaska. The other two are the work of Dayaks in the tropical forests of Sarawak in northern Borneo.

Elaborate woodenwares like these would be used by important people. The old Hawaiian bowl below was the meat-dish or drinking-cup of a chief.

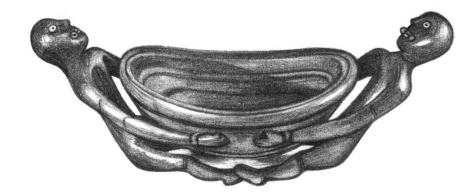

BOWLS WITH HUMAN CARVINGS
Top left: **British Columbia**
Lower left: **Hawaii**
Top right: **Alaska**
Lower left and right: **Sarawak**

SALT DISH
Hawaii

Another old Hawaiian vessel, fit for a chief's household, is supported by figures of stocky acrobatic men standing on their hands. It was probably used as a salt dish.

CUP (*two views*)
Taiwan,
Paiwan people

This cup, with three legs shaped like human heads, is for drinking millet beer. It comes from the Paiwan people of southern Taiwan, who were feared in the past as headhunters. Besides the heads, the cup has carvings of deer, people, and a big coiled snake. Snakes are very common in the mountainous Paiwan country and they are held in awe by the people.

For a wedding celebration the Paiwan make a special double cup—two small cups carved from a single length of wood. The bride and bridegroom must drink together, side by side, and not a drop of the beer must be spilled!

The little pigs, carved on the ends of this cup, are a reminder that roast pork is a food for feasts. Every marriage cup is decorated in a different way; the one shown on Pages 4 and 5 has human figures carved at the ends.

The woman's figure at the right is also a cup, the work of an African carver in Zaire. Like the goblet opposite, this cup is for drinking palm wine.

Fine pots for milk are made by the cattle-herding peoples of East Africa—Somali, Turkana, and Pokot.

Above and opposite:
WINE CUPS
Zaire
Below: **MARRIAGE CUP**
Taiwan, Paiwan people

MILK POT
**East Africa,
Somali people**

To Pokot people milk is more than just food and drink. It can be a holy thing. At a wedding the bride and bridegroom and guests are sprinkled with milk as a blessing. Although some of the Pokot live in settled homesteads and farm the land, many are wanderers, following their herds of cattle. Their few possessions must be easy to carry. Pokot women, as well as men, may carve the wooden milk pots—large ones for adults and little ones for children. The lids

and carrying handles are of leather, decorated with colored beads and strips of aluminum. The rich smoky smell of the pots results from daily cleaning with hot wood ashes, which also gives the milk a smoky taste.

These milk vessels are as simple and practical in their design as the rice bowls carved by the Bontoc

VESSELS FOR MILK
East Africa
Opposite:
Somali people
Left: **Pokot people**

31

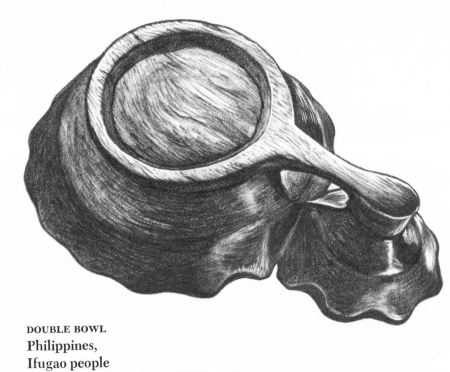

DOUBLE BOWL
Philippines,
Ifugao people

FOOD BOWL
Philippines,
Bontoc people

people of the Philippines. Along with their neighbors, the Ifugao, the Bontoc are well known for their arts of wood and for their rice farming in the mountains of northern Luzon. Their ancestors long ago carved the steep slopes into tiers of narrow terraces. Here the rice is planted, year after year, and springs up in bands of brilliant green around the flanks of the hills.

Besides bowls for rice, the black woodenwares of the Bontoc and Ifugao include spoons of all sizes, and these too can be works of art.

32

ladles, spoons, and dippers are household necessities, even in places where people prefer to eat with their fingers. While many wooden spoons are plain, there are many with decorated handles, and a human head, or a whole human figure, is a favorite design. We can find spoons of this pattern carved by

LADLES
Philippines
Left: **Bontoc people**
Right: **Ifugao people**

34

the Ifugao, the Paiwan, and the American Indians. The fine old Indian spoon at the right was meant to be carried in a man's belt when he was traveling. Many Indian spoons, like the two at the left, were made with hooked ends to fit over the edge of a wooden soup bowl, so that the spoons would not drop into the soup. The squirrel and partridge carved on these two show that the owners belonged to the squirrel and partridge clans.

Among the Indians of the Northwest Coast a man's clan animal would be carved on the special ladles he used for serving food at feasts. You can see one of these on page 1. It was made by a Tlingit carver in Alaska and bears the head of a raven.

CARVED SPOONS
Opposite, left to right:
Philippines, Ifugao people
Taiwan, Paiwan people
American Indian, Oneida people
Right: **American Indian,**
Wyandot people

35

LADLE (*back and front views*)
Siassi Islands, Papua New Guinea

At feasts in New Guinea, big scoop-shaped ladles are used to stir and serve the ceremonial pudding. This one, made on an island off the eastern end of New Guinea, has a design on the back that combines the forms of man and fish. The wood is blackened and the carved lines are painted white.

A common everyday food-stirrer, whether it comes from Africa, America, or the Pacific islands, is usually shaped like a small canoe-paddle, but a good wood-carver will decorate it in any way he likes.

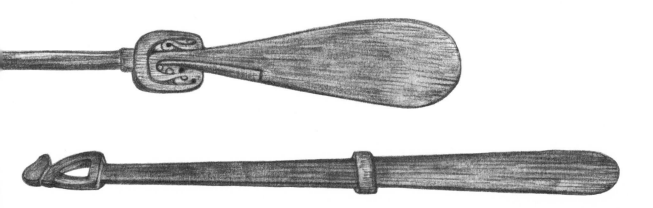

FOOD PADDLES
Above: **Trobriand Islands, Papua New Guinea**
Right: **Surinam**

In the Bush Negro villages of Surinam, in South America, almost every man is a skilled carver, and every household has woodenwares of different design! These people are descendants of black African slaves, who escaped from the plantations along the coast of Surinam and found freedom in the forest. The rebel slaves settled along the great forest rivers; and today the Saramacca people on the Surinam River, and the Djukas along the Marowijne, still follow some of the old ways of their African forefathers.

Not long ago this specially elegant food-stirrer was carved by a young man of the Djuka people as a present for his wife. When they got married, he was supposed to make her a dugout canoe for river travel, as well as all the wooden things needed for proper housekeeping. She would want a fine rice tray, a board for grinding peanuts into peanut butter, a handsome washboard for scrubbing clothes by the river, and of course, a carved stool.

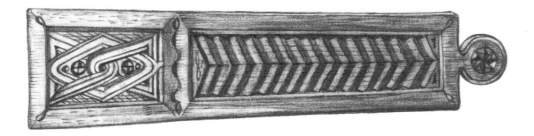

RICE TRAY
AND WASHBOARD
Opposite:
PEANUT BOARD
AND FOOD-STIRRER
Surinam

39

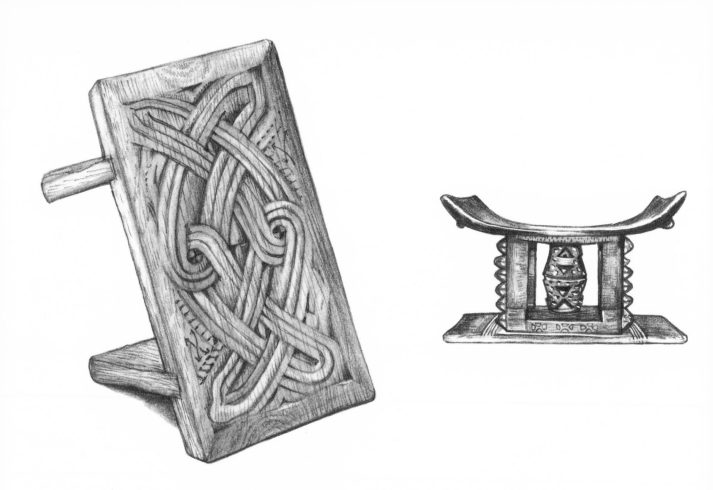

Left: **Surinam,
Djuka people**
Right: **Ghana,
Ashanti people**

stools made by the **Djuka people in Surinam** are as varied in design as their food-paddles. The one above is a woman's stool. To prevent an evil spirit from sitting on it in the owner's absence, the stool has been carefully tilted on end, an old custom that came to the Djukas from their West African ancestors, the Ashanti.

Stools have a very special place among the Ashanti. The symbol of the Ashanti people is the Golden Stool. Their rulers are enthroned on stools, and everyone—man, woman, and child—has a personal stool, designed and decorated according to the rank of its owner. There are different patterns of stools for men and for women, for priests and for royalty.

Among the Lobi, another West African people, a graceful three-legged stool is a sign of manhood. Only after a boy has become a man is he allowed to have a stool like this one and to carry it hooked over his shoulder.

MAN'S STOOL
**Upper Volta,
Lobi people**

The simplest kind of stool—a round seat on a round base—is quite easy to carve from a log of wood, if the carver has a sharp adze and a little skill. The small stool opposite, still bearing the marks of the carver's tool, has four legs between base and seat, rather like human legs bent at the knee. The artist of the African stool has turned the simple round design into a fine piece of sculpture. The figure of a woman supporting the seat represents one of the ancestors of the chief for whom the stool was made.

On the South Pacific islands, chiefs were very often the only people to sit on stools; everyone else

COCONUT-GRATING STOOL
Papua New Guinea

42

sat on mats on the floor. Stools like the one opposite should be called kitchen utensils rather than seats. They are still in use on islands where coconuts grow

43

COCONUT-GRATING STOOL
Lamu, Kenya

and people use coconut in cooking. To get the meat out of a coconut you sit astride the stool and scrape the half-coconut against a jagged shell or a metal knife, mounted on the long projecting neck.

Coconut-grating stools are also used in East Africa by the Swahili people of the Kenya coast. The old one above, with its elaborate carving, is hinged in the middle and folds up when not in use.

The small stool at the right is also from East Africa, from the country of the Pokot people, where only the men have stools. This one belonged to an old man

44

who was a farmer, not a wandering herdsman like many of the Pokot. You can tell this by the shape of his stool.

An old man of the cattle-herding Pokot made the stool below, according to custom, with three splayed legs. Though both stools are small and easy to carry, that of the farmer has an extra advantage. Turned upside down, it becomes a sturdy headrest that he can use as a pillow when he wants to sleep at night or in the heat of the day.

OLD MEN'S STOOLS
(*two views of headrest-stool*)
Kenya, Pokot people

BEADED HEADREST
Kenya, Pokot people

headrests often take the place of pillows when people wear elaborate hairdressings. Pokot men and their Turkana neighbors cover their hair with a thick cap of hardened mud, which is painted blue and sometimes adorned with small white ostrich plumes. Young Pokot men take great pride in their appearance. An essential part of a man's equipment is the spindly little headrest that dangles from his hand by its leather handle. Each man carves his own and usually decorates it with bright beads.

Turkana warriors also carry headrests, but theirs

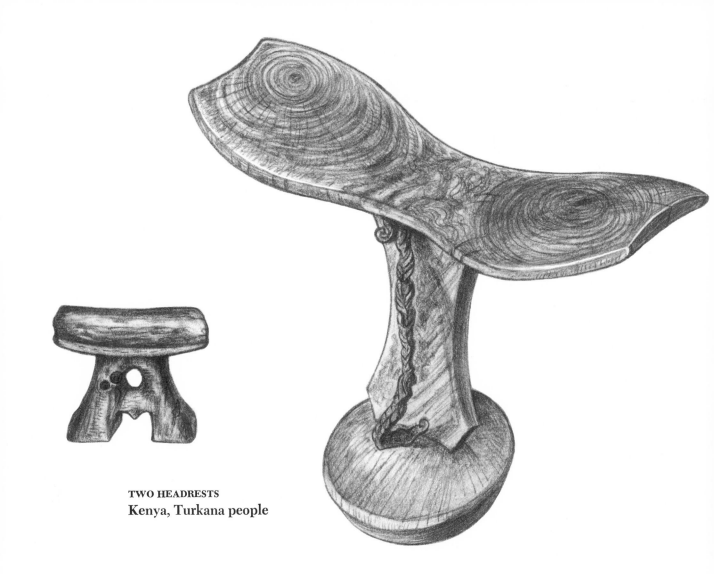

TWO HEADRESTS
Kenya, Turkana people

are generally made in a T-shape. This large one has been carved with a fine feeling for the form and grain of the honey-colored wood.

The Somali people of East Africa make small

lightweight headrests with gracefully curved tops and sides. The one below has a carving of guns and a scorpion on the top, a sort of prayer in pictures. The man who sleeps on the headrest prays for safety from the guns of his enemies and the stings of the big scorpions that come out at night.

The headrests opposite—from Africa and New Guinea—each have a carved human figure to support the top. Sometimes an animal is the supporter, or the whole headrest is made in animal form.

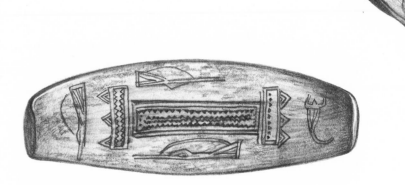

HEADREST
(with view of carving on top)
East Africa, Somali people

48

HEADRESTS WITH
HUMAN SUPPORTERS
Above: Siassi Islands,
Papua New Guinea
Below: Zaire

49

This splendid "chieftain's pillow" from northern New Guinea has ends shaped like the open jaws of crocodiles. It was used in a *haus tamboran*, the great painted house where sacred things are stored, and where the chief and the men of his tribe will eat, sleep, talk, and prepare for ceremonies.

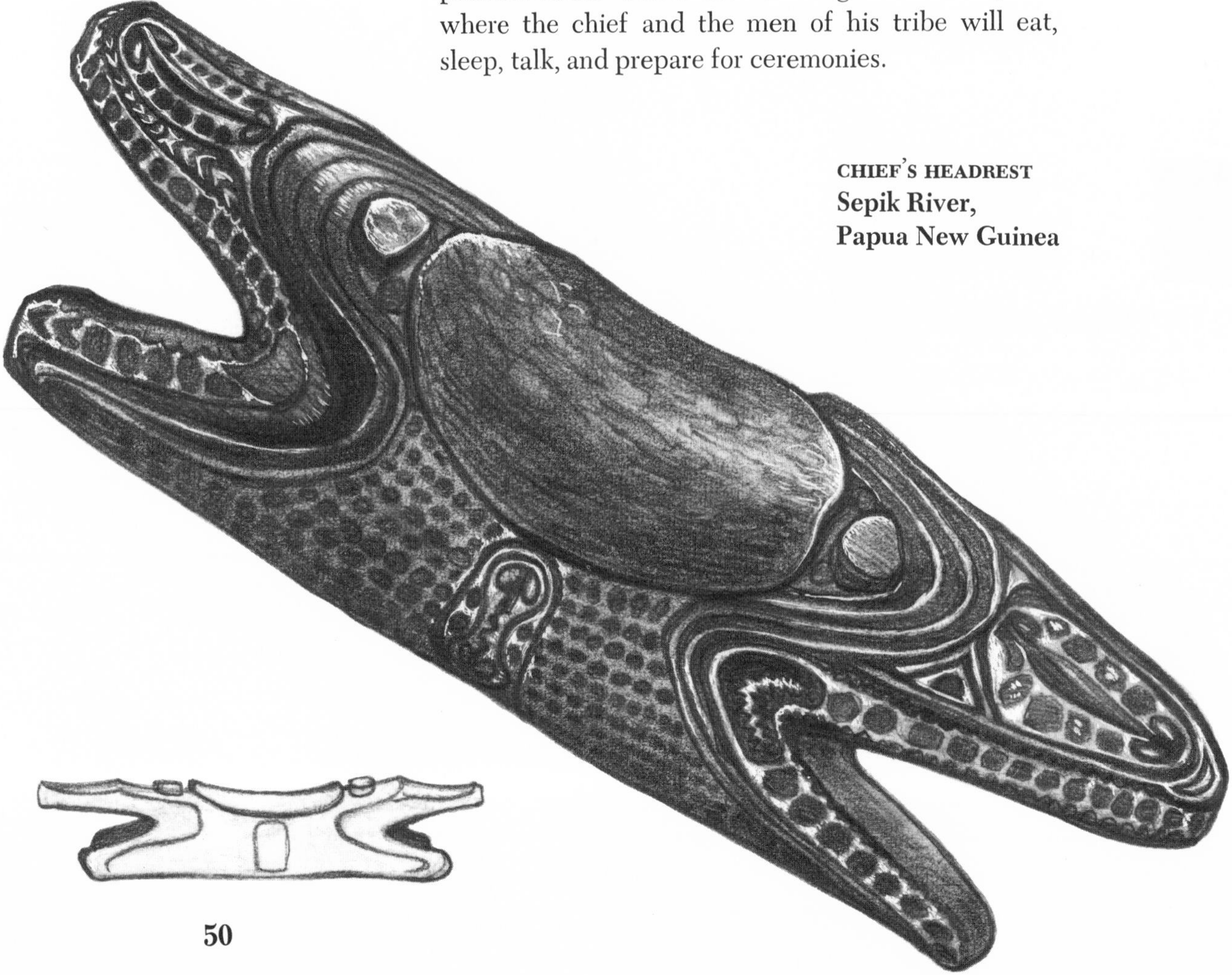

CHIEF'S HEADREST
Sepik River,
Papua New Guinea

50

COMBS
Left: **Ghana**
Right: **Taiwan**

combs, like headrests, are important to people who want to make themselves beautiful. A wooden comb should be strong but also pleasant to use, and if it is carved by a man for the woman he loves, it can become a work of art.

A Paiwan carver may decorate the comb with two twining snakes. An Ashanti comb from West Africa is topped by the head of a woman. The combs

51

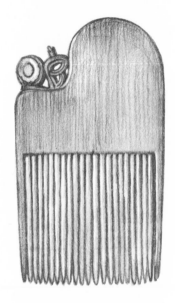

COMBS
Left: **Surinam**
Above: **New Zealand**
Right: **Alaska**

carved by the Bush Negroes of Surinam are the most varied of all. Their ribbonlike, interlacing patterns carry hidden meanings and speak a message to the woman who uses the comb.

A fierce-looking raven, inlaid with shell, adorns a Tlingit Indian comb, which is similar in shape to the comb made by a Maori artist of New Zealand, far south across the Pacific.

The Maori are as well known for their woodcarving as the Indians of the Northwest Coast. Their arts of wood, large and small, are richly decorated with patterns of spirals, human figures, and fantastic beasts.

The small "feather box" below was made to hold the valuables of a Maori chief, including the precious red feathers he wore for ceremonies. This kind of box would be hung from the rafters of the chief's house, and as it was seen from below, the best carving was usually on the bottom.

CHIEF'S FEATHER BOX
New Zealand, Maori people

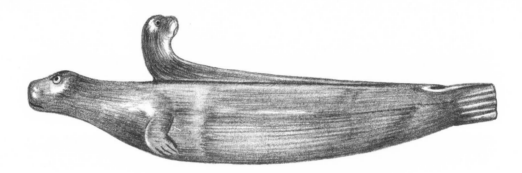

tobacco boxes and pipes for smoking, lime containers and all the equipment for chewing betel nut—these small things can be masterpieces of the carver's art. For many American Indians, tobacco smoking was an ancient tradition, but it was unknown to the Tlingit and their neighbors on the

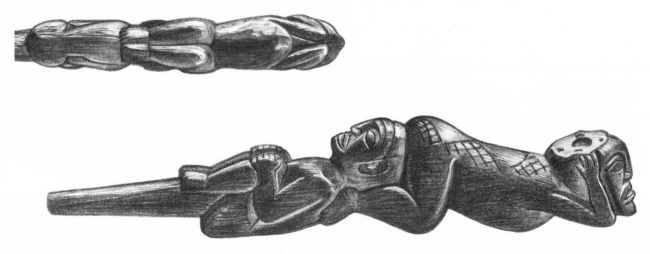

Northwest Coast until white men sold them tobacco. Then, in the hands of Tlingit artists, the wooden bowls of pipes became miniature sculptures of birds, beasts, and people. The Eskimos—always fine carvers of animals—made little tobacco boxes in animal form. The one opposite is a mother seal with her baby on her back.

Decorated pipes are also made by the Paiwan people across the Pacific. The pipe at the left, more lavishly carved than most, has the opening of the bowl in the top of the man's head. Besides using tobacco, the Paiwan chew betel nut, a habit that takes the place of smoking for many people in Taiwan, the Philippines, Southeast Asia, and parts of the South Pacific.

Opposite: **PIPE**
(*two views*)
Taiwan, Paiwan people
Right: **PIPE BOWL**
Alaska, Tlingit people

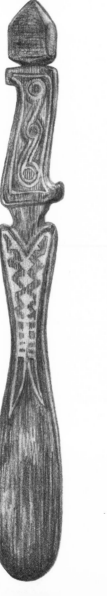

The essential ingredients for chewing are the nut and a pinch of powdered lime. The supply of lime is often kept in a handsome wooden container and served out with a stick or a little carved spatula like a flat spoon. The large lime container on Page 2, made from a dark brown, polished coconut, has two long sticks to go with it and is meant to be shared by several people.

The famous wood-carvers of the Trobriand Islands make big lime spatulas, like the one opposite and the fine one on Page 59, for use on ceremonial occasions, for gifts, and for trade. They also carve the little

Left and opposite:
THREE LIME SPATULAS
Papua New Guinea
Below: **LIME CONTAINER**
Solomon Islands

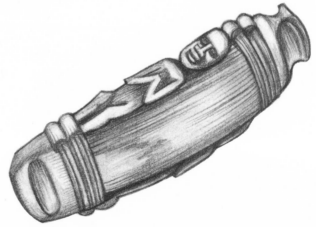

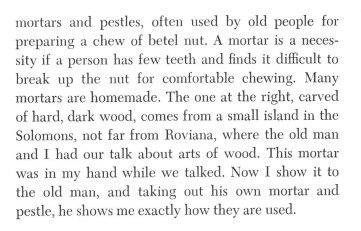

mortars and pestles, often used by old people for preparing a chew of betel nut. A mortar is a necessity if a person has few teeth and finds it difficult to break up the nut for comfortable chewing. Many mortars are homemade. The one at the right, carved of hard, dark wood, comes from a small island in the Solomons, not far from Roviana, where the old man and I had our talk about arts of wood. This mortar was in my hand while we talked. Now I show it to the old man, and taking out his own mortar and pestle, he shows me exactly how they are used.

57

Into the mortar he puts a piece of peeled nut, a folded green leaf, and a pinch of lime. Then he pounds all this to a soft paste with the pestle, scoops the mixture into his mouth, and begins to chew.

By now the patter of rain has stopped, and watery sunlight floods between the trees. We get up and walk through the village, past the brown leaf-thatched houses to the beach, where the dugout canoe that brought me to the island is waiting to take me away. We wade out to it through the warm shallows. Some women are setting off in another dugout, cutting the water with their carved paddles.

I say good-bye to the old man and watch him go back to the village, which lies strung out along the shore below the green forest. Then I look down at the little mortar in my hand, smooth and old and worn. Out of the living trees men have created arts of wood, simple things made beautiful. These are the arts that no one calls "art," because they are as much a part of life as the craft of the housebuilder, the skill of the fisherman, or the swift passage of a dugout canoe across the great lagoon.

Opposite: **BETEL-NUT
MORTAR AND PESTLE**
Left: **LIME SPATULA**
**Trobriand Islands,
Papua New Guinea**

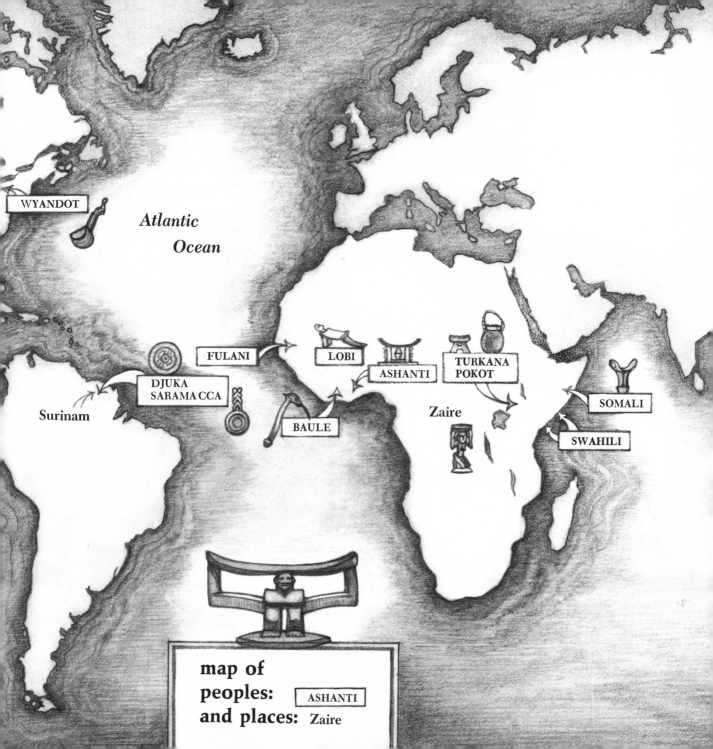

WYANDOT

*Atlantic
Ocean*

FULANI

LOBI

ASHANTI

**TURKANA
POKOT**

SOMALI

**DJUKA
SARAMA CCA**

Surinam

BAULE

Zaire

SWAHILI

map of
peoples: ASHANTI
and places: Zaire

ESKIMO

TLINGIT

TSIMSHIAN

NOOTKA

SAUK

ONEIDA

Pacific

Ocean

PAIWAN

Taiwan

Hawaii

BONTOC
IFUGAO

Philippines

Papua New
Guinea

Solomon
Islands

DAYAK

MAORI

New
Zealand

Sepik River

Siassi
Islands

Papua New
Guinea

Tami Islands
Trobriand
Islands

Collingwood Bay

List of Illustrations

The names of some museums and collections are abbreviated as follows: American Museum of Natural History, New York—AMNH; Author's Collection—AC; British Museum, London—BM; Museum of the American Indian, New York—MAI; Smithsonian Institution, Washington, D.C.—SI; Collection of Vermont State Craft Center, Middlebury, Vt.—VSCC. (Page numbers appear in **bold** type.)

figures. Alaska, Lower Yukon River, Eskimo. Collected in 1845. Length: 9 in. Museum of Anthropology and Ethnography, Leningrad. (*bottom*) Two bowls, with supporting figures. Sarawak, Kenyah people (Dayaks). Sarawak Museum, Kuching. **26** Bowl supported by three figures. Hawaii, 19th century. Height: 8 in. BM. **27** Cup with relief carvings (two views). Taiwan, Paiwan people. Height: 5¼ in. VSCC. **28** Cup in form of woman. Zaire, Bawongo. Height: 7½ in. BM. **28–29** Marriage cup. Taiwan, Paiwan people. Length: 27 in. VSCC. **29** (*left*) Goblet with carving of frog. Zaire, Bushongo. Height: 19 cm. Musée Royale de l'Afrique Central, Tervuren. (*right*) Milk pot, blackened wood carved in low relief. East Africa, Somali people. Height: 34 cm. Musée de l'Homme, Paris. **30** Bowl. East Africa, Somali people. Height: 4½ in. VSCC. **31** (*left*) Man's milk pot with leather lid and handle, decoration of beads and aluminum strips, made by the man who used it. Kenya, Agricultural Pokot people. Height (without handle): 8¾ in. VSCC. (*right*) Child's milk pot with similar decoration, made by the child's mother. Kenya, Pastoral Pokot people. Height: 7½ in. VSCC. **32** (*left*) Double bowl. Philippines (Banaue, northern Luzon), Ifugao people. Length: 10¾ in. VSCC. (*right*) Food bowl with carved animal head. Philippines (northern Luzon), Bontoc people. Length: 5¾ in. VSCC.

ladles, spoons, and dippers

    33 (*left*) Ladle with head carved on handle. Philippines, Bontoc people. Length: 11 in. VSCC. (*right*) Large dipper. Philippines, Ifugao people. Length: 11¾ in. VSCC. **34** (*left*) Spoon with squatting figure on handle. Philippines, Ifugao people. Length: 6⅝ in. VSCC. (*center*) Spoon with standing figure on handle. Taiwan, Paiwan people. Length: 8⅛ in. VSCC. (*right*) Two spoons with partridge and squirrel carved on handles. American Indian, Oneida people, Wisconsin, 1825-1875. Length: approx. 8 in. Cranbrook Institute of Science, Bloomfield Hills, Michigan. **35** Spoon with woman's figure on handle. American Indian, Wyandot people, Upper Sandusky, Ohio, 1799. Length: 8½ in. MAI. **36** Food ladle for feasts, blackened wood with white paint. Siassi Islands, Papua New Guinea. Length: 28 in. VSCC. **36–37** Food paddle. Trobriand Islands, Papua New Guinea. Length: 32⅝ in. VSCC. **37** (*top*) Food paddle. Trobriand Islands. Length: 25 in. VSCC. (*bottom left*) Carved handle of food paddle. Surinam, Saramacca people. AMNH. (*bottom right*) Carved handle of food paddle. Surinam, Djuka people. AMNH. **38** (*left*) Peanut grinding board. Surinam, Saramacca people. Length: 14¾ in. Herskovits Collection, Northwestern University, Evanston, Illinois. (*right*) Food stirrer. Surinam, Djuka people (carving in Saramacca style). Length: 17⅛ in. VSCC. **39** (*top*) Rice tray, worn carving with traces of blue paint. Surinam, Djuka people. Diameter: 24 in. VSCC. (*bottom*) Washboard, relief carving painted in blue, red, and white. Length: 22⅝ in. VSCC.

stools

    40 (*left*) Woman's stool. Surinam, Djuka people. Height: 7½ in. AC. (*right*) Woman's stool. Ghana, Ashanti people. Height: 38 cm. Ghana Museum, Accra. **41** Man's stool. Upper Volta, Lobi people. Length: 20 in. VSCC. **42** Coconut-grating stool, legs bound to top with cord of coconut fiber, shell attached for grating. Papua New Guinea. Length: 27½ in. VSCC. **43** (*left*) Round stool. Kanganaman, Middle Sepik River, Papua New Guinea. Height: 6½ in. VSCC. (*right*) Chief's stool with human supporter. Zaire, Luba people, about 1900. Height: 20½ in. BM. **44** (*top*) Coconut-grating stool with metal grater. Coast of Kenya, Swahili people (carving in style of town of Lamu). Length: 93 cm. Fort Jesus Museum, Mombasa, Kenya. (*right*) Combined stool and headrest, used by old man. Kenya, Agricultural Pokot people. Height: 5½ in. VSCC. **45** (*left*) Three-legged stool, made and used by an old man. Kenya, Pastoral Pokot people. Height: 7 in. VSCC. (*right*) Stool shown on page 44 inverted for use as headrest.

headrests

    46 Young man's headrest, decorated with leather, beads of black, white, blue, and orange, copper and aluminum wire. Kenya, Pastoral Pokot people. Height: 7½ in. VSCC. **47** (*left*) Small headrest. Kenya, Turkana people. Height: 5 in. VSCC. (*right*) Large headrest, handle of plaited leather. Kenya, Turkana people. Height: 7 in. VSCC. **48** Headrest and detail of the carving on the top. East Africa, Somali people (collected in Mombasa, Kenya). Height at center: 5½ in. VSCC. **49** (*top*) Headrest with human supporter, painted in grey, red, and white. Siassi Islands, Papua New Guinea. Length: 15 in. VSCC. (*bottom*) Headrest with human supporter. Zaire, Mbala people. Length: 10¾ in. BM. **50** Chief's headrest, relief carving with white and reddish paint. Sepik River area, Papua New Guinea. Length: 32½ in. VSCC.

combs

    51 (*left*) Comb. Ghana, Ashanti people. Length: 7⅛ in. VSCC. (*right*) Comb. Taiwan, Paiwan people. Height: 2⅛ in. AC. **52** (*left*) Comb. Surinam, Djuka people. Length: 14¾ in. VSCC. (*center*) Comb, inlaid with shell. New Zealand, Maori people. Height: 4¾ in. Cambridge University Museum of Archaeology and Ethnology, Cambridge, England. (*right*) Comb, cedarwood inlaid with abalone shell. Alaska, Tlingit people, 1860–1890. Height: 5½ in. University Museum, Philadelphia, Penn. **53** Chief's feather box, relief carving painted with ochre. Length: 16¾ in. Field Museum of Natural History, Chicago, Illinois.

tobacco boxes

and pipes

    54 (*top*) Tobacco box in form of seal and young, beads inlaid for eyes. Alaska (St. Michael), Eskimo, 1874. Length: 9½ in. SI. (*bottom*) Pipe (views from below and from side), blackened wood with metal around opening of bowl. Taiwan, Paiwan people. Length: 8 in. VSCC. **55** Cedarwood pipe bowl. Alaska (Wrangell Island), Tlingit people, 1850–1875. Height: 8½ in. MAI. **56** (*left*) Lime spatula, relief carving filled in with pink coloring. Collingwood Bay, Papua New Guinea. Length: 8⅝ in. VSCC. (*center*) Lime spatula with incised design. Trobriand Islands, Papua New Guinea. Length: 9¾ in. VSCC. (*right*) Lime container with human figures carved on the sides. Malaita, Solomon Islands. Solomon Islands Museum, Honiara. **57** (*left*) Large lime spatula with carving of two women. Trobriand Islands. Length: 20 in. VSCC. (*center*) Betel mortar with bird carving. Eastern Papua New Guinea, probably Trobriand Islands. Height: 3¾ in. Museum of Science and Art, Buffalo, New York. (*right*) Betel mortar. Vonavona, Western Solomon Islands. Length: 6⅜ in. Solomon Islands Museum, Honiara. **58** Betel mortar and pestle, worn carving of human head on handle of pestle. Trobriand Islands. Length of mortar: 5⅜ in. Pestle: 7⅞ in. VSCC. **59** Ceremonial lime spatula. Trobriand Islands. Length: 12⅛ in. M. H. de Young Memorial Museum, San Francisco, California.